Catholic Poems

from the

Heart of a Red Dirt

Oklahoma Girl

by

Donna Sue Berry

Edited by
Eugenia Hochstedt

Berry Books Publishing

BBP

Berry Books Publishing
PO Box 30661
Edmond, Oklahoma
73003

ISBN 978-0-692-13320-0

DEDICATED

to the

Most Sacred Heart of Jesus

and the

Sorrowful and Immaculate
Heart of Mary

ACKNOWLEDGEMENTS

To my Family and Friends who have suffered through
my rhyming and rhyming, and more rhyming
for so many years.

To Jeremy and Monica Ingle, who
in 2010, gave me my 'first' byline in
The OREMUS PRESS Newspaper,
and whom I have been writing for ever since.
http://www.oremuspress.com/

To Dan Burke, who told me back in 2012,
in Livingston, Montana that he liked my poems
and published some on his Spiritual Direction website.
https://spiritualdirection.com/

To Harry and Beverly Stevens:
Beverly is Editor of Regina Magazine
In 2013, I asked her if she would read one of my poems,
she did, and she liked it.
Soon I was honored to write for them!
https://reginamag.com/

I have been privileged to write
and learn from some of the best!

Special *Thank You* to Eugenia Hochstedt,
who has grabbed her coffee and edited and edited!

She's just an Oklahoma girl
With red dirt in her blood
Born in a Catholic family
Whom she so dearly loves

THE POEMS

Oh, Jesus my Savior,
my Lord, and my King,
You are my God,
my everything!

dsb

I Am Waiting Here for You

Caught up in life and troubled thoughts,
I could not see the faces,
Of people whom I bumped into,
Like I was running races.

With things to do, deadlines to meet,
I did not need distractions,
Nor condemnation for my haste
Or thoughtless, selfish actions.

But in my ear I heard a shout,
A voice out of the blue.
**"Child, stop with all your running, Stop!
I'm waiting here for you."**

I quickly paused and turned around,
Not a soul was next to me,
Just a sign that read "I'm waiting here",
Nailed to an old oak tree.

I hurried on, but in my haste,
I couldn't help but wonder,
About the loud voice in my head
That sounded just like thunder!

"STOP NOW! I'm waiting here for you!"
I stopped and turned to glare,
At an ancient Catholic chapel,
Just beyond a wooden stair.

The chapel seemed to call me,
Though no more words were said,
So, I crossed the pretty garden spot
Toward the church ahead.

Before me hung a wooden sign,
"I am waiting here for you."
Why not, I thought, I'll go inside
And sit down in a pew.

I stepped into the house of God,
I smelled the strong incense,
And quickly fell upon my knees,
My body growing tense.

Upon the altar, standing there,
A monstrance with the Host.
I bowed down low before my God,
The Son, and Holy Ghost.

My heart vibrated with His words,
"Been waiting here for you."
I told Him of my many trials,
And how I loved Him, too.

A blanket seemed to cover me,
With sweet and gentle peace.
Then all the things that bothered me,
Just seemed to fade and cease.

A tender love infused my heart,
I sat in silent prayer,
In adoration and in love,
Without a single care.

Much later as I rose to leave,
My spirit all renewed,
I felt His words within my heart,
"Be waiting here for you!"

©2014 Donna Sue Berry

AS HIS CHILD I WAS NOT LOST

Outside the ice and snow blew hard,
As I lay warm in bed.
Harsh winter winds whipped bare tree limbs
Like drumbeats in my head.

Wrapped in quilts I sat up and peered
Through the window at the scene,
So deep in prayerful thoughts of God;
How small a child I seemed.

While winds tore 'round, my thoughts did too,
Of times I drowned in sin.
Then ice cold tears from pain and past,
Made slow trails down my chin.

Yet a smile played there beneath my tears,
As His child I was not lost,
For God had given all His love
And hadn't count the cost!

©2012 Donna Sue Berry

O BLOOD OF JESUS

I knelt before the Eucharist,
My head bowed deep in prayer.
My thoughts turned toward His agony,
Of pain so hard to bear.

His crimson blood and salt filled tears,
And tortured ragged breath,
The sinful life I'd led for years,
Played out before his death.

Oh, Blood of Jesus flowing down,
Upon the cross upon the ground.
You drop like tears on Mary's hand,
And sink into Golgotha's sand.

O Bread of Life, O Gift of Love,
You come to us from Christ above.
Nailed to a tree from wounds you seep,
And prove your love with each heartbeat.

In thanksgiving then I bowed once more,
Before the Holy Host,
Before the Triune Father God,
Son and the Holy Ghost.

Before the Cup of Precious Blood,
Poured out to give me life,
My Jesus come to save my soul,
Beyond all sacrifice.

O Blood of Jesus flowing down,
Upon the Cross, upon the ground.
You drop like tears on Mary's hand,
And sink into Golgotha's sand.

O Bread of Life, O Gift of Love,
You come to us from Christ above.
Nailed to a tree from wounds you seep,
And prove your love with each heartbeat.

WHERE TWO HEARTS
BEAT AS ONE

The very moment she said "Yes",
Redemption had begun.
The prophecies of old fulfilled,
Where two hearts beat as one.

The Spirit overshadowed her,
Because she had believed.
As heaven met with earth that day,
The God man was conceived.

God's son, her son, became a man.
This Rose of Sharon's bud,
So soon to bloom upon the cross,
He'd shed His flesh and blood.

In Bethlehem, a stable blessed,
Saw angels sheer delight,
Where first she held Him to her heart,
That cold and starry night.

At the wedding feast in Cana,
Came the miracle; a sign.
He would not deny His mother,
As water turned to wine.

On the Via Dolorosa,
Then up to Calvary's hill,
Walked two hearts as one united,
And bent to do God's will.

His words that "It is finished" made
The sacrifice complete.
She saw His spirit leave Him and
His heart no longer beat.

They placed her son into her arms,
And pain tore her apart.
Remembered words of Simeon,
The sword had pierced her heart.

But came the dawn of Easter morn,
Veiled meeting with her son.
The prophesies of old fulfilled
Where two hearts beat as one.

MASS OF ANCIENTS

Gold candlesticks are shining,
As the altar's all aglow,
So starts the Mass of ancients,
As angels bow down low.

While the choir intones its high chant,
The procession's drawing nigh.
Rose incense rising upwards to
Our mighty God on high.

The solemn altar boys approach,
With Crucifix in hand,
They trail before the celebrant,
His vestments gold and grand.

Only moments now await us,
Before the Consecration,
Then "Ecce Agnus Dei"
As we kneel in adoration!

THE CONFESSION

The moment I woke up I knew,
That this would be the day,
I couldn't bear it anymore,
So I began to pray.

The world, the flesh, and the devil,
Had lied to me again,
They'd led me down the primrose path
Of avarice and sin.

Without the grace to persevere,
I'd not be there in time,
So, I raced off to confession,
Just as the church bell chimed.

The line was full of people and
I stood there for so long,
While guilt and sin weighed down on me,
From things that I'd done wrong.

But when it came my time to go,
I entered and knelt down,
Father raised his hand in blessing,
His words a welcome sound.

Then "Go ahead," was all he said,
So I unloaded all my pain,
And listened as he spoke to me
God's mercy once again.

The words, "Ego te absolvo . . ."
Made tears run down my chin,
As he poured on me God's mercy,
Forgiving me my sin.

©2015 Donna Sue Berry

O MOST SACRED HEART OF JESUS

It wasn't for the first time that I'd stepped inside to pray,
The church was cool and empty, and I had so much to say,
But I barely said I love you, when tears began to fall,
I tucked my face inside my veil, and waited for it all.
When at last my sobs subsided, I raised my head to see,
The most Sacred Heart of Jesus, was there in front of me.

"O Sacred Heart of Jesus,
I kneel before Your throne.
I pray You wrap me in Your arms,
And take me as Your own!
Make my poor heart to beat like Yours,
In union as if one,
Where want, and need, and worry melt,
And sin becomes undone.
Most Sacred Heart of Jesus,
You have loved us all so much,
Now grant that I may live for You,
And honor You as such!"

©2015 Donna Sue Berry

OUR PARISH PRIEST

Long days and nights are what he spends,
As shepherd to his flock,
Of souls who need his tending care,
Sometimes around the clock.

It's early every morning when
He hits his knees to pray,
Late nights prostrate upon his face
He wrestles in the fray.

Each day upon the altar stone,
He offers Sacrifice,
Christ's very Flesh he gives to us,
And Blood that paid the price.

Each moment of the day not his,
Not in the very least,
His time is filled with saving souls,
This is our parish priest.

©2014 Donna Sue Berry

HE IS MY PRIEST, ONE OF MY SONS

"NO!" Mom said, "Don't you ever talk about a Catholic Priest."
You lift them high and pray for them, an Ave in the least!"
"Oh, fine." I muttered to myself and headed for the door.
Our parish priest was such a grump, so harsh, and quite the bore!

Now here it was late Saturday; confessions start at three.
Oh, man, I hoped it'd not be him who would be hearing me.
But when in the confessional, his words were kind yet strong.
With compassion, love, and mercy, he absolved me from my wrongs.

With humbled heart and sin freed soul, my penance I then prayed,
But just as I began to leave, I felt the need to stay.
So, I sat down in the shadows, alone there in the church,
When suddenly a noise up front caused my body such a jerk!

My priest had dropped a kneeler, and he knelt on it to pray.
His body bent with burden, and emotions just gave way!
My parish priest was weeping; much like a child he seemed,
Not the harsh and grumpy cleric, whom I had wrongly deemed.

Then light circled around him, and a shadow I could see.
Was that a man or angel, who stood there in front of me?
As I peered into the darkness, it all became quite clear,
It was the Lord, the Son of God, who wiped away his tears.

With His hands upon his shoulders, then Jesus whispered "Rest."
And Father sank against His Heart, his head upon Christ's chest.
But as Jesus stood behind him, He looked toward my way,
"This is My Priest, one of My sons, of whom I ask you pray."

His words were barely spoken when He disappeared from sight,
The peaceful look upon his face, showed Father's burdens light.
And as he stood, he saw me there, then gave a nod and smiled,
But as he left, I knelt back down, to pray for him awhile.

©2012 Donna Sue Berry

THAT LITTLE CATHOLIC BOX

Out to dinner with some girlfriends, conversation turned quite deep.
Then one spoke up quite boldly for an answer she did seek.
Why do you go in early to this thing that you call Mass?
Why wear that 'thingy' on your head and do an hour fast?

And what about that little box, where you go to tell your sins?
We're all just so confused about this church that you are in!
Then in silence they sat waiting, to hear what I would say,
I whispered in a coward's voice, "It's just our Catholic way."

But driving home I passed my church, and hung my head in shame.
Just as St. Peter realized, I, too, denied His name.
I spent the night in restless thought of what I should have said,
My Savior, Jesus, died for me and for my sins he bled.

I should have said, quite frankly, I believe that He is there,
Upon the altar in the flesh, a sacrifice laid bare.
To receive Him in Communion, the Church says I must fast,
An hour without food or drink, is not that much to ask.

I wear a scarf upon my head, in reverence to my King,
Where in solemn worship it is His praises that I sing.
I go early for the reason, to examine sin and know,
To receive an absolution, I must prepare my soul.

It's all these things I should have said, in answer to my friends,
So they would know my Catholic faith, this church which I am in.
And what about that little box where I go to tell my sins?
You can bet tomorrow morning I'll be there and going in!

©2011 Donna Sue Berry

PRAY IT!

"NO!" I screamed at the car windshield,
Though I could barely catch my breath.
Not another tragedy but
The news confirmed more death!

"This world has gone to hell!" I thought,
As I shook my head and sighed.
Can we even stop this madness?
Then my rosary caught my eyes.

Around the mirror hanging there,
Swiftly swinging to and fro,
As if to say "I am waiting,
And the answer's here you know."

Our Lady said to pray it and
To pray it every day,
For peace to reign throughout the world,
Her rosary we must say!

So I pulled into a parking lot,
From the mirror grabbed my beads,
And bowed my head to kiss the cross
As I began the Creed . . .

TO YOUR ROSARY I CLING

Queen of the Holy Rosary,
My Queen and Mother too,
I'm kneeling here in tears today,
And asking help from you.

There's more than just a raging storm,
I'm lost and all alone,
I need your help to pick me up,
From where my life's been thrown.

I'm holding to your promises,
To your rosary I cling,
While winds of sin whip me around,
And rip my soul and sting.

Please help me to a life of grace,
From hell where I have been,
Back to the arms of Jesus Christ,
Where life is free of sin.

©2012 Donna Sue Berry

THE OLD WOMAN WITH HER ROSARY

I nearly knocked the old woman down,
When I pushed the church front door,
But swiftly said, "I am sorry",
With my eyes glued to the floor.

I quickly turned my face away,
And tried to hide my tears,
Didn't need the woman's pity,
Nor the 'wisdom' of her years.

So, I bent my head in silence,
Underneath the chapel veil,
My poor heart completely broken,
As my soul began to wail.

Crumbled up there in the church pew,
I had never cried so much,
And I never heard her coming,
Til I felt her gentle touch.

Not one word did she say to me,
She just handed me her beads,
In her eyes a look of knowing,
As she slowly turned to leave.

While I clutched her rosary tightly,
I could feel the smooth worn glass,
And I whispered all the 'Aves'
As I waited for the Mass.

Then my soul began to quiet,
As my pain began to ease,
With the promise of her Rosary,
I felt our Lady's peace.

©2015 Donna Sue Berry
Ad Majorem Dei Gloriam

THE WEATHERED OLD
VIRGIN STATUE

The weathered old Virgin statue,
Next to the garden stairs,
Stands in silent witness to
So many whispered prayers.

Wrapped up in frozen stillness,
As sleet is raining down,
Icicles form around her like
An icy winter gown.

The arctic winds and frigid cold,
The worst this year has seen,
Blast frosty, crystal snowflakes on
Her chilly Majesty.

She appears an icebound sculpture,
As blizzard winds have blown,
Crystallized and set for winter,
In ice-cold concrete stone.

THE YOUNG WARRIOR'S PRAYER

A rosary clasped tightly in his little hands,
A small little guy with a spiritual plan,
His worries were big as he knelt by his bed,
While thoughts of his daddy kept filling his head.
"My son", Dad had whispered, "I'm counting on you.
Take care of your mom, and take care of you, too!"
His dad then left for the war, he went far away,
But Mamma had taught him to hope and to pray.

In PJs and tee shirt, his bear by his side,
He prayed each Hail Mary and tried not to cry.
With a cross as his shield, and beads as his sword,
The young warrior's weapons could not be ignored.
"Hail Mary," he pleaded, "help me understand.
Please, bring Daddy home from that far away land."
The Mother of Jesus heard this sad little boy,
So, she asked her own Son to fulfill his joy.

And answer God did, one bright sunny day,
No more going to war, he'd come home to stay.
The boy ran to his daddy; his tiny feet flew.
Picked up into arms, "I've been waiting for you!"
He welcomed Dad home with his rosary in hand,
And hugs, tears, and kisses from his little man.

©2013 Donna Sue Berry

THE LITTLE CATHOLIC SHRINE

I sought shelter in the little shrine, inside from falling rain.
Away from all my crosses and away from all my pain.
October's angry storm outside no way compared to mine,
As I knelt within the shadows of the little Catholic shrine.

I could smell the burning incense left from the morning Mass,
While I watched the candles melting on their candlesticks of brass.
With the sound of rolling thunder, I knelt in great despair,
By the statue of our Lady, then I began my prayer.

"I am begging Blessed Mother; come help me please today.
My life is all in shambles and my faith has gone astray.
I ran from Jesus long ago; I hid my face in shame.
I no longer have the strength inside to call upon His name"

The Statue seemed to smile at me, I felt a calming touch,
From the Mother of my Savior, whom I had missed so much.
I could almost hear her heartbeat; her message was complete.
As she held a set of rosary beads with three kids at her feet.

"Say the Rosary every day, this way there will be peace.
Now call upon the Name of Christ, and let your worries cease!"
I grabbed my rosary, closed my eyes and prayed for me and mine,
Then stepped out into the sunlight from the Little Catholic Shrine.

©2012 Donna Sue Berry

Our Lady of Fatima
Pray for us

THE OLD WOMAN AND HER ROSARY

The old woman and her rosary,
I see her every day,
So deep the pain within her eyes,
She grips it tight to pray.

It is her dear companion,
Her best friend in time of need,
Old fingers dance in silent prayer,
Then slide from bead to bead.

She thinks upon its mysteries,
Christ's life upon this earth,
Of her old age and wasted days,
And what her life is worth.

About her youth and bygone years,
When she was taught this prayer.
So glad to be in "Mary's" hands,
Wrapped up in her wheelchair.

Throughout her day she prays for souls,
For those whom she knows not,
That grace and mercy fall on them,
And they are not forgot.

In tattered robe and old house shoes,
Soft habit which she wears,
She offers up her daily pain,
With every whispered prayer.

My sweet Mamma and her rosary,
I see her every day,
With faith in God deep in her eyes,
She grips it tight to pray.

I love you, Mamma

OUR LADY OF FATIMA

It has been over a hundred years,
Since Mary came to us.
And now it's worse than it was then,
With sin and godless trust.

Our Lady told the children,
Pray the rosary every day.
For conversion, peace, and mercy,
It would save the world this way.

We must always pray her rosary,
It's what we need to do!
For the Pope, our Church, and family,
Our friends and Poor Souls, too.

©2016 Donna Sue Berry

MAMMA'S ROSARY

I remember Mamma's rosary, it was always in her hands,
With her fingers working quickly across the beaded strands.

With the words of each Hail Mary, her worries fell away,
As she'd go about her housework and sanctify her day.

With trust she'd always grab them when things would go astray,
Mixing rosary beads and tear drops, as silently she'd pray.

She could pull one out of nowhere, and they seemed to multiply.
As she'd pass one out to each of us, we dare not roll our eyes!

It's funny, now years later, as I sit with her in Mass,
I spy the same old rosary beads she holds upon her lap.

There's a peaceful look of Heaven as she prays on every bead,
With her total trust in Jesus supplying all her needs.

But when that day shall come, I dread, when she is here no more,
I'll pray those special rosary beads just as she had before.

©2011 Donna Sue Berry

THE ROSARY ON THE HEADBOARD

I stumbled through my daily grind,
Right up until midnight,
Fell into bed without my prayers;
I knew it wasn't right.

I was so tired, almost asleep,
When thoughts kept waking me,
To rise and pray a rosary
Upon my bended knees.

But my rosary beads were knotted,
Around my headboard rail,
And tired attempts to pull them down,
Ended to no avail.

"Our Lady knows how tired I am,"
Was my last waking thought,
"Should she want me to pray her beads,
Then she'd untie the knot."

Then suddenly I heard a sound,
As I began to snore,
My rosary beads unwound themselves,
And landed on the floor!

I quickly slid down to my knees,
A humbled shameful heap,
And prayed our Lady's rosary beads,
In meditation deep.

Much later as I crawled in bed,
My rosary in my grip,
I shut my eyes and fell asleep,
Hail Marys on my lips.

©2014 Donna Sue Berry

Our Souls, They Are Not Dead

In silence late one evening, I found myself alone,
Enjoying for the moment some peacefulness at home.
A steamy cup of coffee with a shot of Irish Cream,
Had lulled me into comfort as I drifted off to dream.
The mistiness around me draped my shoulders like a shawl,
While voices so familiar seemed to beckon with a call.

"Pray for us, please, pray for us, and offer up your pain.
We need your acts of charity to fall on us like rain.
Please, sprinkle holy water, light a candle in our stead,
For we long to see our Savior; our souls, they are not dead!"

Stunned, I peered in silence as I strained to hear each sound,
From the shadows there before me, as I knelt on holy ground.
Daddy? No, my grandpa? Was that my late but dearest aunt?
Did I hear the voice of family in their soft and pleading chant?

"Pray for us, please, pray for us, and offer up your pain.
We need your acts of charity to fall on us like rain.
Please, sprinkle holy water, light a candle in our stead,
For we long to see our Savior; our souls, they are not dead!"

Their entreaty begged compassion, with a plea for so much prayer,
That I quickly sought the Face of God to ask Him then and there,
'For the Souls in Purgatory, dear Father, grant release,
That soon their cries are silenced when at last they dwell in piece.

Still if my dad therein resides or my grandpa and my aunt,
Please, take them soon to Heaven, of this I ask you grant.'
That is when I made a promise, to pray and not forget,
My family who may need me still to help repay their debt.

Their voices slowly faded; I could barely hear their call.
Quiet darkness overtook me, then I began to fall.
But with a start, I jumped in pain! Hot coffee on my pants,
Yet still, it seemed, I heard the sound of Poor Souls as they chant.

"Pray for us, please, pray for us, and offer up your pain.
We need your acts of charity to fall on us like rain.
Please, sprinkle holy water, light a candle in our stead,
For we long to see our Savior; our souls, they are not dead!"

©2011 Donna Sue Berry

I Have Been Here for a Long Time

I have been here for a long time,
As you can surely see.
All friends and family dead and gone,
None left to pray for me.
If only I had known in life,
What waited past death's door,
I would have sacrificed and prayed,
More than I had before.
I did just what I had to do,
At least that's what I thought.
But now I see that I fell short,
From what the Church had taught.
These Purgatory pains are real,
The Father's gift of grace,
A time to cleanse myself from sin,
So, I can see God's Face.
My contrition was imperfect,
My heart and will so frail,
Without these cleansing holy fires,
I would end up in hell.
So, if by chance, you read these words,
Please say a prayer for me,
That soon my soul is spotless and
The Father's face I see.

A Cemetery in Montana

In the middle of Montana,
Off a dirt road on a hill,
Stands a graveyard so forgotten,
Where the dead are sleeping still.

The ground is cracked and broken from
The heat of summer's sun,
Like the souls in Purgatory,
Whose sufferings are not done.

While they thirst there for our kindness,
They long to see God's face.
But now can't fly to heaven,
Nor leave behind that place.

With their bodies in Montana,
Their souls beseech our prayer,
For only us still living can
Relieve the pain they bear.

"Oh, Father, send a storm of grace,
Let it fall like morning dew.
Rain down on them forgiveness,
For the punishment that's due.

Cleanse their souls, remit their debt,
Let them kneel before Your throne,
So, they may praise and worship in
The glory of Your home."

Prayers for the Dying, Prayers for the Dead

Again, it seemed a rainy day
Had led me to a dream,
My rosary wrapped around my hand
And coffee full of cream.

As I settled with a book to read
But drifted off to sleep,
I found myself within a fog
Upon a rocky heap.

It seemed the stones around my feet
Were used to mark a grave,
And posted as a warning to
The entrance of a cave.

I peered into the darkened hole,
But only saw pitch black,
And then I heard a mournful sound,
Which made me jump straight back.

Such cries, pleas, and frightening sounds
That made my blood run cold,
I quickly crossed myself and prayed
St. Michael's prayer of old.

Suddenly, the air grew still as
A light shown in the night,
An Angel beckoned me to kneel
And pray with all my might!

"Someone is dying," were his words,
 "so near the gates of hell.
Pray hard now for his salvation,
Before they ring death's bell!"

I threw myself upon the ground,
Prostrate before the Lord,
And fought for his conversion with
My rosary as my sword.

I begged God's Divine Mercy with
My arms stretched open wide,
And prayed he'd find repentance
And forgiveness as he died.

It seemed I prayed for hours,
Doing battle for his soul,
When lightning struck across the sky,
And closed that deep dark hole.

Then scores of angels shouted,
"Alleluia!" to their King!
As Purgatory opened in
A mighty rushing swing.

A soul was saved, God's grace revealed,
But no time yet to rest,
A time of expiation due
This soul who had been blessed.

Reparation, prayers, and masses now,
To quench him from the fires,
To see the Holy Face of God,
Is what the law requires.

So, in charity and kindness,
Please, pray for those who've died,
That soon they see the golden gates
Of Heaven open wide.

When They Come to Me

They always seem to come to me, just when I fall asleep.
As the darkness overwhelms me, into my mind they seep.
They're the faces of my loved ones, yet some I've never known.
They push and pull into my dreams; some plead, some cry
or moan.

"You have the chance to kiss our Lord,
Each day at Holy Mass.
Yet waste your time on worthless things,
No thoughts your life will pass.

But pass it will, then you'll be judged, in truth before the Lord.
Condemned for all eternity? Or Heaven your reward?
But what if you, like us fall short, before the Face of God?
Will you, like us, regret the times your prayer life was so flawed?

Listen now, and see our pain, please pray for our release.
Then we, in turn, shall pray for you your love of God increase.
Waste not your time, for it grows short, but sacrifice and pray!
We ask for your indulgence to reduce our debt away."

With that they usually disappear,
I kneel in silent prayer,
That soon they see the Face of God,
With no more debt to bear.

THE SHEPHERD GIRL'S CHRISTMAS

Bethlehem town was sound asleep,
As were the little lambs.
So, she spread her tiny blanket out
To rest upon the sand.

But just as she began to nod,
She opened up her eyes,
To see the stars in heaven dance,
With Angels in the sky!

As she stared in fascination,
Her heart began to stir.
Then an Angel stood before her,
And spoke to her these words.

"Young shepherd girl, come quickly, run,
There's someone you should see.
Don't fear the dark of night my child,
Come quickly, come with me!"

She followed him into a cave;
Beheld a sight of joy,
As Angels hovered reverently
Around a baby boy.

The baby looked into her eyes,
She felt her knees grow weak.
She knelt beside the manger crib,
And kissed his tiny cheek.

At once, she understood the tales,
About the baby King,
Who'd come to earth to save mankind,
And take away death's sting.

She felt the need to fly and tell,
The others on the hill.
Her Angel smiled as if to say,
"Go child, it is God's will!"

Then off she ran into the night,
To shepherds whom she knew,
So she could tell about the child,
And they could worship, too.

"My shepherd friends, come quickly!
There's someone you should see.
Don't fear the dark of night my friends,
Come quickly, come with me!"

***** ***** *****

Words spoken on that starry night,
Two thousand years ago,
Now joyfully bear repeating in
The Advent candle's glow.

As you kneel before the Eucharist,
Can you hear the Angels sing?
"Come see the child of Bethlehem,
Come see the Risen King!"

THE CERAMIC NATIVITY SET

In the darkness of the closet,
Where no one else could see,
There sat a hidden manger scene,
My Mom had given me.

On the shelf above the linens,
Pushed back and out of sight,
I never had to look at it,
When I turned on the light.

You see my Grandma had made it,
She sculpted it by hand,
With gentleness had painted it,
The reddish hue of sand.

But I didn't like to see it,
It always made me cry,
Reminding me of Grandma,
And others who had died.

At Christmas Mom would set it out,
Our focus for advent,
And not the gifts and toys we got,
Nor money we had spent.

The manger scene reminded us,
Through the Advent Season,
The holy child of Bethlehem,
Jesus was the reason.

So it sat there shelved in darkness,
Just hidden from my sight,
Until one of my grandchildren
Had asked me late one night,

"Why is Jesus in the closet?
I looked at him surprised,
As his finger pointed upwards,
With excitement in his eyes.

I turned and looked upon the shelf,
The manger scene had moved,
No longer hidden from my eyes,
But sitting in full view!

I stood and looked in disbelief,
I alone knew it was there.
"How on earth did it move forward?"
All I could do was stare.

Then my grandson muttered "Angels."
And wandered off to play,
While my mouth flew open wider at
What I had heard him say!

So, I reached into the closet,
Pulled down the manger set.
I placed it on the tabletop,
So we would not forget.

Those we've loved, who've gone before us,
Are never really gone.
It's through our kids and grandkids that
Their memories live on.

That this tiny little baby,
Through the Christmas Season
The holy child of Bethlehem,
Jesus is the reason!

True story. Many years, ago when we were little, our Grandma Lorene Stander, (Mom's mamma) made the ceramic nativity set for our family. Our Mom would always put it out the weekend after Thanksgiving to start the Advent season. This is my tribute to our Grandma Stander; may she rest in peace. Thanks for the memories, Grandma! My grandson, Ryan, was the toddler who was sitting at my feet when I was getting sheets out of the linen closet that night, and when he looked up and saw the nativity set...well, now you know the rest of the story.

CHRISTMAS FROM THE CHOIR LOFT

I sat in my festive crinoline dress,
On a chair in the loft of the choir.
The Schola all joyfully harmonized
As their song grew much louder and higher.

Adeste Fideles swirled 'round in my head,
As the candlelight danced in the church.
My eyes were quite glued to the manger below
As I viewed from the heights of my perch.

The crib was quite empty, except for the straw,
But the shepherds were gathered around.
And Mary and Joseph stood waiting there, too,
While the animals slept on the ground.

Jesus was coming, and the Priest had said so,
As he spoke before Mass had begun.
Excited I waited, with my hands folded tight,
For the birth of God's own tiny son.

The Mass was so long, that I closed my tired eyes,
Hoping soon the Christ child would arrive.
And Jesus did come as I dreamed dreams of Him,
Though I slept as the Host was held high.

Much later as Daddy carried me out,
I saw the baby asleep on the hay.
And I thought to myself as I fell back to sleep,
I would see him again the next day!

I COULD BE YOU

I drove right through the changing light,
Horns blowing as I went.
I had to make just one more store,
Before the day was spent.

I swerved in time to miss a man,
Who held a cardboard sign,
A homeless man, who'd work for food,
Thank God, I'd braked in time.

I parked my ride and looked around,
Then groaned at what I saw,
A sea of cars parked everywhere;
The world was at the mall.

Oh, Lord, I thought, it comes again.
The season of excess.
When want and greed are king and queen,
And reign in selfishness.

Then smiling wide, I grabbed my purse.
This was my time to shop,
And for the homeless on the street,
I had no time for thought.

But just outside the store front door,
A homeless woman sat.
She was dirty and disgusting,
With a child upon her lap.

She looked at me with pain filled eyes,
She seemed to read my mind.
"I could be you," she mouthed the words,
"Some place, some other time."

I turned my head, I walked right past.
My conscience now was sore.
With every purchase that I made,
I'd see her at the door.

Then passing by a manger scene,
I stopped to stare awhile,
For the Virgin and her baby
Were the woman and her child!

Remembering that pain filled look,
And how she'd read my mind,
"*I could be you,*" she'd mouthed the words,
"*Some place, some other time.*"

With no more thought, I turned around,
My Christmas I would share!
But the woman and her baby,
They were no longer there.

Just a note upon the sidewalk,
A scribbled cardboard sign,
"*I could be you*", she wrote to me,
"*Some place, some other time.*"

CHRISTMAS THEN AND NOW

Way back then we had no money,
Yet we didn't know it,
It wasn't quite the focus and
Mama didn't show it.

Our simple life at Advent time,
Couldn't seem much stranger,
To those who watched our joy filled looks,
At that empty manger.

How we waited on the Savior til
Those midnight Mass bells rang,
Though we didn't know the lyrics,
Our little voices sang.

It was ALL about the baby,
The Christ child sent to earth,
The Blessed Virgin's little boy,
The night she gave Him birth.

But somewhere in the future,
The focus all got lost,
It became about the party,
No matter what the cost.

The thrills, the bills, and the burdens,
Took the place of simple joy,
Soon anticipation was not
About the Virgin's boy.

As our lives became much harder,
And forced us to our knees,
Looking at the empty manger,
Produced a tearful plea.

"Lord, make of me a child again,
Who seeks the simple joy,
Of looking t'ward the straw filled crib
To find her baby boy."

THANK YOU, GOD, FOR JESUS

I truly now can say to you,
As Christmas drifts away,
This was an Advent to remember,
And a special Christmas day.

Our families all had fasted;
Had petitioned God for grace,
With what a joy to see at Mass,
The peace on each one's face!

With four weeks of preparation
And sacrifices made,
We came to place our gifts of straw
Where Jesus would be laid.

Each piece of hay an offering,
A penitence of love,
It was all to welcome Jesus,
The Christ child from above.

The church was filled with candles;
An ethereal kind of light,
While the choir sang out like angels,
Just before it turned midnight.

When he spoke the consecration,
"Father, Son, and Holy Ghost"
The anticipation ended,
As Father raised the Host.

"Thank you, God, for Jesus,
And thank You for His birth.
We thank you for the time he spent,
Those years upon this earth.

But mostly now, we thank you, God,
He rose up from the dead,
That we may feast each day we live,
On Consecrated Bread.

THE BUSINESS WOMAN'S
LOST CHRISTMAS

She sighed and locked the office door then headed for the car,
Her face turned toward the sleet like mist and saw the shooting star.
'How strange', she thought to see a star on such a stormy night,
It shone with such intensity, a mystical kind of light.

If she were just a child again, she'd make a wish to believe,
And feel the way she used to feel, this night on Christmas Eve.
It wasn't that she was unhappy, nor wished her life would change,
But where was the joy she used to feel when Christmas morning came?

She drove into the silent night, slow through the icy blast,
Her thoughts on many childhood dreams and ghosts of Christmas past.
Ahead she saw a little church, and heard its church bells ring,
She slowed the car, and then she stopped before the manger scene.

She saw a tiny little girl, alone just standing there,
Reminding her of someone in her coat and curly hair.
Stepping down into the drifting snow, and up behind the child,
She couldn't see the young girl's face, but knew that she had smiled.

The little girl stretched out her hands to the baby in the hay,
It happened then a miracle still talked about today.
The plastic Jesus lying there, at once, became alive,
Reaching out his tiny fingers to the girl of almost five.

The woman knelt in disbelief; the little girl turned 'round,
And looking into *her own eyes*, she knew whom she had found.
Then suddenly it all came back, the joy which she had lost,
Because the baby lying there, for her had paid the cost.

The little girl then smiled and waved, slowly fading in the mist,
As the woman bent her head to leave Jesus with a kiss.
Then off she drove into the night, a child again reborn,
Filled with the joy and happiness that comes each Christmas morn.

Merry Christmas!

A KING AMONG KINGS

Brought by three kings who followed a star,
Three gifts for the baby they sought for so far.

At the sight of the three, Joseph, Mary, and Son,
They knew they'd arrived; this babe was the one!

At once they fell down; deep in silence adored,
The child in his blankets; the infant, their Lord.

Gold, frankincense and myrrh, they offered oblation,
Gifts for the newborn, to show their elation.

So solemn their homage; the Magi could see,
His birth for mankind; an epiphany!

This manifestation, for Gentile or Jew,
Christ, King among Kings,
The Savior brand new!

©2012 Donna Sue Berry

THE SWEETEST HEART OF JESUS

From the corner of my church pew,
Sometimes I feel alone,
When I see the happy couples
In love when I'm alone.

I hide behind my lacy veil,
And duck my head to pray.
I wish this year was different on
This 'Sweethearts' special day.

I look up past the altar rails,
I see the Sacred Heart,
His eyes full of affection and
My tears begin to start.

His Mother stands there next to Him,
Her heart is set on fire,
With love for all her children,
And I feel a sweet desire.

A warmth invades my senses as
I feel a 'special' grace,
From the Sweetest Heart of Jesus
Like a kiss upon my face.

©2014 Donna Sue Berry
Valentine's Day

COME LAY YOUR HEAD
AGAINST MY HEART

Come lay your head against my heart,
I'll bathe your soul with peace.
It's time you learn to trust me child,
Let all your worries cease.

My Blood was spilt to save your soul,
I washed away your sin.
Now open up your heart to love,
Allow your Savior in.

'My yoke is sweet, My burden light.'
You've read the words before.
Take up your cross, come follow me,
My grace on you I'll pour.

My Precious Blood will be your drink,
For food you'll eat My Flesh.
When everlasting life has come,
It's you I will caress!

Let Saints of old proclaim the truth,
My Flesh and Blood are life!
So eat and drink for you shall live,
To rise above this strife!

LENTEN ASHES

There's purple on the altar?
Oh, no! What did I miss?
I'm still celebrating Christmas,
Enjoying all my gifts!
But I open up my Missal,
The index is quite clear,
Three more Sundays til Ash Wednesday,
Already Lent is here!
With forty days to change my life,
Forty days to fast and pray,
I'll seek to love Almighty God,
And change my sinful ways.
Starting with the cross of ashes
Father places on my head,
I'll make out a list of penance
To keep beside my bed.
So, with purple on the altar,
Repentance in my heart,
Bring on the prayers and fasting,
I can't wait for Lent to start!!!

©2012 Donna Sue Berry
Lent Septuagesima Sunday

WHAT WILL YOU GIVE?

A friend of mine said Lent was here,
Then asked what I'd give up.
I smiled and told her, "I dunno,
How 'bout my coffee cup?"

But all day long they haunted me,
The words I'd said were trite,
And when I fell asleep I knew,
It'd be no normal night.

I dreamt myself within a crowd,
That stunk and smelled of shame,
Who screamed and shouted death to him,
A man they didn't name.

They shoved me over cobblestones,
And up a rocky hill,
Just in time to see him fall,
The man whom they would kill.

His bloody face and countenance,
Brought tears into my eyes,
But I couldn't find compassion,
In the crowd of passersby.

Then from the ground he looked at me,
Reached out his bloody hand,
That's when I found myself alone,
Before the man condemned.

"What will you give?" I heard him ask,
My soul he seemed to see,
I fell beneath his bloody gaze,
And cried, "I give up me!"

©2005 Donna Sue Berry
January, 29th, 2005

OUR LADY'S FIRST SORROW

The Prophecy of Simeon

O Simeon, O Simeon, what prompted you to say,

Those sad words you spoke to Mary, which made her cry that day?

When you saw the Virgin Mother, with Jesus her newborn,

Did you perceive the bloody Cross, Nails, and the Crown of Thorns?

As she climbed upon the temple steps, was your soul set on fire?

Could you hear the loud "Hosannas" sung by an angel choir?

Then lifting him into your arms according to the law,

Was it the Lord Almighty in the tiny face you saw?

Did her joy turn into sorrow as you talked about the Lord,

And how someday she'd suffer with her soul pierced by a sword?

But as they turned and walked away, did it become quite clear,

Our sins would nail him to that cross and cause our Lady's tears?

© 2017 Donna Sue Berry

OUR LADY'S SECOND SORROW
The Flight into Egypt

"Arise and take the baby
To Egypt with his mother,
Fly far from here, and don't look back,
But travel undercover."

As the Angel spoke to Joseph,
He woke him from his rest,
He warned him of the peril to
The babe at Mary's breast.

Though Joseph saw the danger in
What lay for them ahead.
He knew that if they stayed behind
His son would soon be dead.

So that night they left for Egypt,
No one knew that they had gone.
No one knew that they were fleeing,
Long before the break of dawn.

He quickly took his family,
Far from their holy home,
Far from their Jewish culture and
The lives which they had known.

Into a land they'd never seen,
So full of history.
Into the Land of Pharaoh where
God set the Hebrews free.

Saint Joseph would protect them there,
With angels by his side,
And live in humble poverty
Until King Herod died.

©2017 Donna Sue Berry

OUR LADY'S THIRD SORROW
The Loss of the Child Jesus in the Temple

Mary's heart kept beating faster, her fear grew deeper, too.
But night turned into morning with still no son in view.
They'd searched all night through caravans, among family and
friends,
But couldn't find their Jesus, and they feared a tragic end.

St. Joseph said, "Let's turn around," their mood anxious and grim.
They started back toward the gate, back to Jerusalem.
Back to the crowded city streets, into the noisy crowd,
Her broken heart preparing her for Christ wrapped in a shroud.

They knew that soon the day would come when he would leave
this earth,
When all of it would come to light, things hidden since his birth.
But now she craved the sight of him, the sound of his young voice;
Back to the temple they would go, they had no other choice.

In temple then, to their surprise, he sat among the men,
With doctors who were listening, who stood in awe of him.
"Son, why hast thou done so to us?" Pained words he heard her
sigh.
Though she'd not understand at all, the words he'd then reply.

"How is it that you've sought me here?" Their confusion must
have shown. "I am about my Father's work,"
Yet he left with them for home.
Back in Nazareth, their holy home, he'd always honor them,
And there in wisdom grow with grace, before his God and men.

©2017 Donna Sue Berry

OUR LADY'S FOURTH SORROW

Mary Meets Jesus Carrying His Cross

As she came around the corner,
She stopped to catch her breath,
Then through the crowd she saw his face,
His pallor quite like death.

Her heart almost exploded as
She then beheld her son,
With his bruised and battered body,
And the torture they had done.

He sunk beneath the heavy cross,
As legs gave way in pain.
A man of massive open wounds,
A lamb that'd soon be slain.

No way for her to get to him,
The soldiers like a wall,
Her ears assaulted by the din,
With horrid, cursing calls.

So, weakened by the loss of blood,
He seemed to stare in space.
But when she moved into his view,
He saw his Mother's face.

For just a moment they could see
Into each other's eyes.
Both felt the pain reflected there,
Each heard their silent cries.

O the thoughts that passed between them,
As soldiers pushed and shoved.
A son and mother sacrifice,
No two more ever loved.

But fleeting moments soon were gone,
They yanked him from her view,
And vanishing into the crowd,
She felt her pain renew.

©2017 Donna Sue Berry

OUR LADY'S FIFTH SORROW
The Crucifixion

While you stood there in the chaos,
Could you see past all the pain?
Past the sword that ripped your own soul,
To your son's triumphant reign?

Did the sands there of Golgotha
Scratch lines into your face,
Mixing with the blood of Jesus,
Dearest Lady, full of grace?

While you stayed beneath his shadow,
While he hung there on the cross,
Could you feel your own wounds bleeding,
As his blood fell to the rocks?

As the turmoil clutched your sad soul,
Did your heart completely break?
Could you hear the soldier cursing,
When his hammer hit the stake?

The *Prophecy of Simeon*,
Had it at last come true,
Where the thoughts of many people
Would lay bare because of you?

Was it when the earth was quaking
That reality set in,
Your son had died to save our souls,
Because of all our sin?

I ask you all these questions as
I'm leading up to one.
Can you forgive me, Blessed Mother,
For the dying of your son?

OUR LADY'S SIXTH SORROW
Mary Receives the Body of Jesus from the Cross

Had it really been that long ago she'd held him in her arms,
And kissed his tiny tear stained face until his heart grew calm?
But now they sat in darkness on a hill they called the Skull,
Where she kissed his bruised and lifeless face, its pallor gray
and dull.

She had known this day was coming, for she'd known it was God's
plan,
That he'd grow up to shed his blood, a sacrificial lamb.
But knowing lessened not the pain, nor quelled her trembling hands,
As she held his body close to hers, her son, God's son made man.

'Oh, sad and sorrowing Mother, your soul pierced by a sword,
It was our sins that killed your son, we crucified our Lord.
Forgive us, now the time has come to lay him in the grave.
We take away your very all. It was your all you gave.'

©2017 Donna Sue Berry

OUR LADY'S SEVENTH SORROW
The Body of Jesus is Placed in the Tomb

Now Sabbath was upon them,
And the air began to chill.
Their tiny group moved quickly as
They started down the hill.

The horror of his sacrifice,
The blood, the nails, and tears,
Would stay with them forever,
To haunt them through the years.

As Joseph offered a new tomb,
Wherein to place her son,
They wrapped him in a linen cloth,
Quite hurried to be done.

But standing there his mournful Mother,
Stayed present til the end.
Though weight from her great sorrow made
Her weary shoulders bend.

Such pain no one has ever known,
As she who gave him birth.
No grief, no sorrow, quite like hers,
Never upon the earth.

With strength, she conquered her desire
To stay within his tomb.
Was grace that prompted her away,
Back to the upper room.

Beside her John and Magdalene,
Not leaving her alone,
But in sadness moved in silence,
While walking Mary home.

VERONICA'S VEIL

Veronica could not compete
With the roaring, raucous mob,
Though no one heard her plea to move,
She pushed with one last sob.

Compassion and persistence,
Had begged her try again,
And just that quick she found herself
Before the man condemned.

It's then He fell beneath the cross,
that forced Him to the ground,
Which ripped His skin and tore His face,
Head pierced by thorny crown.

Blood mixing with the dirt and stones,
They spat upon Him too,
This cursed man whom they reviled,
As winds of hatred blew.

But quickly moving to His side,
She felt a sudden chill,
The world around her disappeared
And time itself stood still.

She slid her veil from off her head,
And with it cupped His face,
A touching act of mercy in
Response to heaven's grace.

Then as she pulled the veil away,
A tear ran down her cheek,
His look of love made her cry out,
And made her knees grow weak.

His sacred eyes, His holy face,
His body racked with pain,
A memory she'd not forget,
Long after He was slain.

But soldiers then wrenched her away,
Into the screaming crowd.
She clawed and shoved her way through them,
Heart pounding with head bowed.

At last she found a quiet street,
And knelt in sheer relief.
The bloody veil clutched to her chest,
She cried from fear and grief.

Then as she held the veil she saw
The imprint of His face,
Majestic in Its blood and wounds,
The source of every grace.

The image burned upon her soul,
She found she could not speak,
But bowed in adoration as
She kissed her Savior's cheek.

THE VEIL

For just a moment she'd been there, directly in His gaze,
And handing Him her linen scarf, He'd wiped His bloody face.
Though her veil was meant to help Him, it caused more pain instead,
By catching on the thorny crown, encircling His head,

In pain He'd handed back her veil, hands shaking as He did,
His eyes expressing tender love through bruised and swollen lids
So captivated by His look, she couldn't hear the sound,
Of the chaos all around her as she knelt upon the ground.

Motionless on the rocky road, her heartbeat nearly stilled,
Recognizing God before her, this man who'd soon be killed.
Suddenly, hard and calloused hands had gripped her upper arms,
Which tore her gaze from off His face, and from that crown
of thorns.

Then flinging her into the crowd, a soldier jeered with glee,
With hatred on his evil face, all she could do was flee.
Once past the cruel and angry mob, she'd still no time to rest,
But had to hide outside the horde, fear building in her chest.

She stumbled to a doorway just as darkness filled the sky,
And crouched beside the wooden door where mournfully she cried.
Emotion overtaking her, she soon began to shake
While trembling fingers held the cloth that wiped her Savior's face.

"O Jesus," was her silent cry, "now what are we to do?
How will we live in dreadful fear or survive without You?"
Collapsing on the stone-cold ground, she shuddered from the chill,
Remembering just how He looked, she tightly hugged her veil.

And staring at the bloody cloth, she ceased to make a sound,
For what she saw upon her scarf made her heart start to pound!
It was her Savior and her Lord, she saw His Holy Face,
Imprinted there upon the veil, a miracle of grace.

The weight of His expression and His agonizing pain,
She knew that she would not forget nor ever see again.
So, she knelt before the image, the icon of her Lord,
She cupped the veil, inclined her head, and bent down to adore.

BEFORE THE LORD

With one swift jerk; I am awake,
Beneath the trees alone.
Not a sound but from a distant crowd,
Who'd from the garden flown.

I'd tagged far behind the Master,
Not wanting to intrude,
But felt the fear rise up in me,
When I saw his somber mood.

I'd watched him kneel, lost deep in prayer,
I'd seen my Master's face,
His blood like sweat dripped down his cheeks,
Like water from a vase.

Then, somehow, I had not kept watch,
But had fallen into sleep,
Now he was gone, and I'm alone,
In fearful misery.

Next fear or grace prompts me to run,
And nightmare turns to day,
I round a corner just in time ,
To see him in the fray!

"Jesus!" I scream but he can't hear,
The frenzy all too loud.
I push and shove until at last,
I'm breaking through the crowd.

"Jesus! Master!" He drops his cross,
And falls upon a knee.
I fall down, too, before my Lord,
And see He looks at me.

Then with one swift jerk, I am awake,
Bowed down in veneration.
Before the monstrance with my Lord,
At church in Adoration.

THE TRIUMPH OF THE CROSS

In the shadow of a doorway,
I hung back behind the swarm,
So, scared by what had happened
As I watched the mounting storm.

Golgotha's hill was covered,
With an ugly, angry crowd,
Some cursed and shouted "Crucify!"
While others wailed out loud.

The air seemed filled with demons,
There was hatred everywhere,
No one moved to stop the madness,
They could only stand and stare.

With the words that "It is finished."
He expired with his last breath,
And satan was defeated at,
The moment of his death.

As thunder roared and lightning struck,
Some graves were opened wide.
The dead arose to witness that
God's only son had died.

The relic shows with evidence,
What's won with his life lost,
Stands still today exalted in
The Triumph of the Cross.

©2014 Donna Sue Berry
September 14th
Exaltation of the Cross

RUN TOWARD THE
GARDEN TOMB

Sweet Mary, hurry fast and run,
Toward the garden tomb.
The sun is rising, I am, too,
From deep within death's womb.

My triumph over sin and death,
Is but a breath away.
Its grip upon My Flesh and Blood
Can't keep Me in this grave.

The time is here, the time has come,
Rise from your grief to see,
I stand here now victorious,
Come see what Angels see.

My kingdom is for you to share,
Forgot not were your tears,
Nor the way that you anointed me,
While some stood back in fear.

My daughter, come, claim your reward.
I live! You hear my voice!
Move quickly to the sound of it,
For you may now rejoice!

So run, sweet Mary, hurry fast,
Toward the garden tomb.
The sun is rising; I am, too,
From deep within death's womb.

My triumph over sin and death,
Is but a breath away,
It's grip upon my flesh and blood,
Can't keep me in the grave!

IN YOUR MERCY, I TRUST

I said I trusted His Mercy,
But in truth, I did not.
My soul and mind, they were so tired,
I found no peaceful thought.

I'd worked so hard to make things right,
Pressures had weighed me down.
But burdens seemed to smother me,
I thought that I would drown.

Then Saint Therese came to my mind,
Her childlike way of trust.
She'd thrown herself into His Heart,
Believed His Mercy just!

She chose His Infinite Mercy,
Remembering she was small,
Into God's arms she fell trusting,
Completely gave her all!

Now is the time, I must let go,
Letting my heart trust Him,
And fall into the arms of God
To breathe His Mercy in.

©2016 Donna Sue Berry

WHAT IS A SAINT?

"What is a Saint?" you ask of me,
"What is it that they've done?"
They lived a life of holiness,
It's Heaven's crown they've won.

The Church has always recognized,
Some for emulation,
The one's whose honor, laud, and praise,
Deserve our veneration.

Heroes and Heroines worthy,
Examples of Christ's love,
Surrendering life and spirit,
To God alone above.

May they intercede for us and
Pray us through to Heaven,
So we may prove triumphant with
The grace that God has given.

©2012 Donna Sue Berry

MOTHER ST. TERESA
of
CALCUTTA

With withered face and folded hands,
her knees worn hard from prayers,
She walked the streets of India
amidst the deathlike stares.

Born Agnes in Albania,
Becoming Indian by choice,
She broke through the hardened social caste,
To give untouchables a voice.

She left the comfort of the convent
to live her calling on the street;
A mission source of charity
To everyone she'd meet.

Calcutta was the new home where
She came with thirteen nuns,
To start the journey of a lifetime
Where her future had begun.

Care for the homeless, sick and dying,
Comfort to victims of disease.
Her heart and hands worked side by side
With loving expertise.

The softness in her voice,
But determination of her will,
Reached far and wide around the world
and reverberates there still.

For the poor to have a peaceful death;
Was core to her belief,
So, those who lived like animals
Could die with angels in relief.

Her death was mourned by millions,
No less those still on the street.
But her sisters live the mission
In the homeless whom they meet.

Though her sari draped bent body,
Always searched there for the poor,
She no longer seeks the needy,
As Teresa stoops no more.

SAINT MONICA, PLEASE PRAY FOR ME

My tears were falling once again,
As I bowed my head to pray.
It wasn't for the first time that
I ran to church today.

In the coolness of the chapel,
I sank down to my knees,
Where pain and disappointment,
Seemed to all but smother me.

My husband and my son were lost,
My life was torn apart.
I fell before the Lord my God,
And I prayed with all my heart.

I looked up to see some relics,
On the wall just left of me,
When one caught my attention,
I moved closer, then to see.

It was Monica of Hippo,
Wife, mother, and so saintly.
I knew her name, but not much else;
Her story only faintly.

Her husband and her son had been,
Scoundrels at their best.
Her constant prayer and fasting,
Had given her no rest.

But in the end, God triumphed,
Her ceaseless prayers were heard,
Such miraculous conversions,
The two of them incurred.

Augustine soon became a saint,
Her husband, too, was saved,
With trust in God I knelt back down,
And promised not to cave.

Saint Monica, please hear my prayer,
My family's gone astray,
You once said, *"Nothing's far from God."*
And so I ask you pray.

Please help their souls, and bring me peace,
Pray heaven be their end.
And as for me, I will prevail,
To be your closest friend.

With that all prayed, I left the church,
My faith in God renewed.
My heart and soul much lighter with
The grace of God imbued.

©2013 Donna Sue Berry

THAT HEART STRING MOMENT

The heat beats down upon me
From the Oklahoma sun,
As I walk into the building
When supper has begun.

I can see their withered faces,
Their purpled, frail, worn hands.
Some sit and stare at nothing,
Or wobble when they stand.

Then I weave through crowded hallways,
Past nods and speechless smiles,
To my mother's tiny bedroom
to sit and chat a while.

Today, she mostly knows me,
And the stories I re-tell,
Like where she is, and why she's here,
Her fears are hard to quell.

Just when my heart starts breaking,
And my tears I cannot still,
Mom reaches out to pat my hand
And whispers, "It's God's will."

©2016 Donna Sue Berry

TODAY I SAW MY MAMMA CRY

Today I saw my Mamma cry,
And couldn't do a thing,
Old tears fell onto wrinkled hands;
Time crushed her with its sting.

So, I held her gnarled fingers,
And kissed her hair of grey,
But she couldn't breech the sadness,
She had nothing to say.

She finally, softly whispered,
In a voice so frail and low.
I miss your Dad so much, she said,
Don't know why I don't go.

As I held her sobbing body,
Old woman meek and mild,
She curled into my arms so tight,
It seemed she was *my* child.

Oh, Mamma, the time is coming,
And coming way too fast,
When I can't hold you anymore,
Or make these moments last.

I love you so dearly, Mamma.
Please, know how much I do.
And when at last you're with my Dad,
I'll be here missing you.

©2015 Donna Sue Berry
I love you, Mom

FROM MY HEART

THE MEMORIAL CARD POEMS

Our Nephews

and

Family and Friends

Eternal Rest, grant unto them, O Lord,
and may Perpetual Light shine upon them.
May their souls, and the souls of all the faithful
departed, through the Mercy of God, rest in peace.
Amen.

*(We know not, of course, who is in Heaven,
but we pray for the souls of all who have died)*

For Jordan

Now rest in peace my Angel,
As you lay within Christ's arms.
You'll never shed a single tear,
Nor fear of any harm.

You'll only know the sweetest touch
Of Heaven's gentle kiss,
My tiny little baby boy,
My child of whom I'll miss.

You crossed over early, Jordan,
Into the Promised Land,
Where the Saints and Angels waited,
And took you by the hand.

They led you to your Papa Bob,
Who kissed your tiny face,
He whispered words of love to you,
In heaven filled with grace.

Your Grandparents, Aunts, and Uncles,
All ancestors welcomed you,
And your sibling who'd been waiting,
Was there to greet you, too.

Then your Guardian Angel Dear,
Dressed you in garments white,
Approached the mighty throne of God,
So brilliant and so bright.

So rest in peace, My Angel,
As you lay within Christ's arms,
You'll never shed a single tear,
Nor fear of any harm.

You'll only know the sweetest touch,
Of Heaven's gentle kiss,
My tiny little baby boy,
My child of whom I'll miss.

©2011 Donna Sue Berry
Requiescat in Pace
Jordan Anthony Leehan
March 13th, 2011

You only lived a few seconds upon this ole earth . . .
but your Daddy Baptized you,
and you are so very loved.

I WOKE UP TODAY
IN HEAVEN

I woke up today in heaven,
And Jesus took my hand.
I didn't need my wheelchair,
I could move my feet and stand.

I heard the sound of Angels
Singing praises to the Lord,
Not the oxygen machinery
Upon the children's floor.

It was then I took my first step,
And I ran for the first time,
Into the arms of Jesus where
He placed his head on mine.

Welcome home to glory, Keaton.
I've been waiting for a while,
To have you here in Heaven
And to see your perfect smile.

I heard a voice call out my name,
I grinned and turned to stare
At my little brother, Jordan, who
Was laughing, standing there.

"Hello, brother." he said to me,
As we hugged for the first time.
"Come on and meet your family!"
Then I looked at that long line.

A man walked up and shook my hand;
He smiled and gave a nod,
Hello, Son, I've really missed you,
I am your Grandpa Bob.

Hey, guys, don't grieve my passing.
I am happy and brand new!
So talk to me, I'm listening,
I am praying here for you.

For
Keaton Alexander Leehan
Requiescat in Pace

March 20th, 1995
July 26th 2013

Baptized and Confirmed at age 2 months,
You suffered greatly for over 18 years,
And, oh, how your Daddy and Mamma
and siblings love you.

THE LOVE FROM GRANDMA'S HAND

The call came in, I had to rush
To be there by her side.
The trip was long, and time was short,
To say my last goodbye.

My Grandma had always been there,
So much a part of life.
To think that she would soon be gone
Cut sharp just like a knife.

So many things I'd like to say,
So many things to ask,
Like before she was my Grandma,
who was she in the past?

A woman of the world they said,
Dined with generals and kings,
A photographer who broke through walls,
Who captured many things!

In Africa she took pictures,
Some not allowed before,
But I knew her as my Grandma
Someone whom I adored.

Out of love, she learned to sign when
My Momma couldn't hear.
My Grandma did so many things
For us that were so dear.

It's all these things I thought about,
As I rushed to Grandma's bed.
But the words, I love you, Grandma,
Were mostly in my head.

I made it to her room in time;
Beside her bed to stand,
And through my tears to kiss and see
The love from Grandma's hand.

For Jonathan and Teresa Vestal with love.
November 16th, 2011

When Jon's Grandmother was passing,
she signed with her hand,
"I love you".

Rest In Peace
Mary Rose Van Scyoc

CLIFF

25 years ago today,
That crisp October night,
Their jeep went spinnin' round the curve,
Cliff's soul flew outta sight.

Brilliant red hair and those freckles,
Cliff's cute yet ornery grin,
Quickly left us without warning,
Such painful loss set in.

Our family lost a member,
A mother lost her son,
Three brothers once together,
Found they were missing one,

Our lives have never been the same,
His leaving left a scar,
Yet brought us closer to our God,
No matter where we are.

Though that night so long ago,
We felt his soul depart,
We trust our God and we believe,
Cliff rests within His heart.

© 2010 Donna Sue Berry

Eternal Rest grant unto him, O Lord,
and may Perpetual Light shine upon him,
and may his soul and the souls
of all the Faithful departed,
through the Mercy of God, rest in peace.

Rest in peace, Cousin.
Clifford Foster

MERRY CHRISTMAS
MY SON

Merry Christmas to you, Merry Christmas, my son,
Although I'm not with you, I am not really gone.
The clouds they may hide me, through sorrow and tears,
Remember I love you, your voice I still hear.

I'm no longer in pain, and I no longer cry,
For God has now healed me, and my tears are all dry.
I am free of my chains that did hold me so tight.
And now I see Jesus, such a wonderful sight.

Remember the good times, please remember my love.
I live now with Jesus, in Heaven above
God made me a mother, and the gift of a son
He gave me the graces to make me your Mom!

So proud of you, Brian, for all that you've done,
You have carried this cross, not so easy my son.
I am right here beside you, and I lift you in prayer.
From Heaven I watch you; no need for more tears.

There's a Mom here in Heaven, who once lost her child,
Blessed Mary's her name, she's so tender and mild.
Hold close to the Savior, He'll take care of you, son.
He'll bring you to me when your work is all done.

Remember the good times, and remember my love,
I live now with Jesus, in Heaven above.
God made me a mother, and the gift of a son,
He gave me the graces to make me your Mom!

©2011 Donna Sue Berry
For Brian Gibbs
Who lost his mom too soon.
Requiescat in Pace, Lisa Gibbs

SALUTE TO MY SOLDIER
SALUTE TO MY DAD

"My Soldier son, you've gone to Heaven,
I know not the reason why,
The reason how it happened,
Or why you had to die.

How can it be that you are gone,
My son and my big man?
I'll salute you always, Damon
And beside you always stand."
Dad

"Hey Dad, I'm standing right beside you, I am never far away.
Just close your eyes and think of me; say what you want to say!
God alone knows why I am here, and why I had to die,
But I remember when you hugged me and the day we said goodbye.
I remember all the laughter; tears when I could not stay.
I remember all my childhood and the games we used to play.
Remember all the tricks we pulled, and Marci's cracking up?
Remember all the jokes we told and my favorite drinking cup?
Oh yeah, for that whole "Snowflake" thing...I'll get you back
somehow,
And though you cannot call me up, I hear you even now.
Aww, Dad, I'm not so far away, just feel my silent touch,
With all my heart, I love you, Dad, you'll never know how much.
I respectfully salute you, too, and beside you stand the same,
It's all because of you, my Dad, I'm the man that I became."

Damon

© 2011 Donna Sue Berry
In Memory of Damon Thomas Leehan
Requiescat in Pace, Soldier
Beloved Son, Husband, and Daddy

1Lt US ARMY
Sept. 11, 1980 - Aug. 14th, 2011
Bronze Star Purple Heart

We will never forget
Operation Enduring Freedom

ONCE in a while, right in the middle of an ordinary life,
LOVE gives us a *Fairy Tale* come true...

TIL I MET YOU

Never met a Catholic Cowboy, who bows his head to pray,
With his Rosary in his pocket, each and every day,
Who whispers to his Father God, from deep within his heart,
When life is full of happiness, or when it falls apart.

This cowboy who loves Jesus Christ, is such a Godly man,
Who sets the course throughout his day, to follow Heaven's plan.
A bull ridin' kind of cowboy, so Catholic and so true,
Never met a Catholic Cowboy, that is til I met you!

©2010 Donna Sue Leehan Berry
February 8th, 2010

FOR JOEL DOC BERRY
"Montana"

Books from my childhood
The reason I write

This little book of poetry is comprised of poems which Donna Sue Berry has written over the years from childhood to now. She has written poetry for The Oremus Press Newspaper, Catholic Spiritual Direction, and Regina Magazine. Some of these poems were written for her four other published books which are, *The Sorrows of the Blessed Virgin Mary, Poems in Honor of Our Lady of Sorrows; Our Souls, They are Not Dead, Poems, Prayers, and Promises for the Poor Souls in Purgatory; Veronica's Veil, Poems, Prayers, and Promises of the Holy Face Devotion; and Veronica's Veil Companion Prayer Book.* Books available in all bookstores, Amazon, and directly from the author.

Donna Sue was born and raised in central Oklahoma in 1955, and is a wife, mother of two, and grandmother of twelve. She and her retired rancher husband, Joel Doc, share their time between the wheat fields of Oklahoma and the mountains of Montana. She began writing poetry and song lyrics soon after she first read Romeo and Juliet during her junior year in high school. However, it wasn't until she enrolled in her freshman year at the University of Central Oklahoma (at age 47) that her poetry began to deepen and truly express her great love for Christ and her Catholic Faith. Donna Sue's favorite poems are rhyming, story poems which weave around a person's thoughts and emotions. She says she writes with an Oklahoman's heart and accent.

All Glory to God

Berry Books Publishing
P.O. Box 30661
Edmond, OK. 73003

catholicpoet@att.net

https://catholicpoemsfromtheheartofareddirtoklahomagirl.com/

www.ingramcontent.com/pod-product-compliance
Lightning Source LLC
Chambersburg PA
CBHW042128080426
42735CB00001B/4